PROFICIENT'S

COMPREHENSIVE GUIDEBOOK AS PER LATEST CBSE SYLLABUS

ENGLISH

FOR CBSE CLASS 10

BY KAMAL SARMA AND BHUBANESWAR SARMA

PROFICIENT

(A COMPLETE COACHING, DEVELOPMENT AND PRACTICE GUIDE)

Borjhar, VIP, Guwahati, Near North East small Finance Bank Branch, Assam, India-781015
Contact No. 9706567627, 9085094195,9101443160, Mail Id-kamalcaedcl@gmail.com

PREFACE

'PROFICIENT's Guide on English, CBSE Class 10' is a comprehensive guide book on English. This book is written under the guidance of the Academic scholars of Proficient Academy. The sole purpose of this book is to extend help and support to the students of 10th standard under CBSE, NCERT curriculum in an affordable manner. We expect that the guidebook will be proved to be fruitful to share in depth knowledge to the students. The readers are requested to send their feedbacks at the mail address of the author, so that we can improve the next edition. This book introduces you to how to present yourself in the examination. This book is not meant for learning the chapters, but to make the students understand the skill how to write the answers in the most appropriate way.

In this first edition 'Proficient' family tries to help the students with NCERT Text book questions only, but no sample paper or summary of the text contents are given in this book. But 'Proficient' is very much committed to improve the contents in the editions to come.

With best wishes to our readers and well wishers.

Authors
Kamal Sarma
Bhubaneswar Sarma

CONTENTS

ENGLISH LANGUAGE AND LITERATURE (Code No. 184)
CLASS – X (2020-21)
SECTION - WISE WEIGHTAGE IN ENGLISH LANGUAGE AND LITERATURE

Section		Total Weightage
A	Reading Skills	20
B	Writing Skills with Grammar	30
C	Literature Textbook and Extended Reading Text	30
	TOTAL	80

Note: The annual examination will be of 80 marks, with duration of three hours. There will be internal assessment for 20 Marks.

PART A (40 Marks)

Reading **20 Marks**

1. Multiple Choice Questions based on a discursive passage of 400-450 words to test inference, evaluation and vocabulary. Ten out of twelve questions to be answered. **(10x1=10)**

2. Multiple Choice Questions based on a Case-based factual passage (with visual input- statistical data, chart etc.) of 300-350 words to test analysis and interpretation. Ten out of twelve questions to be answered. **(10x1=10)**

(Total length of two passages to be 700-750 words)

Literature Textbooks **10 Marks**

1. Multiple Choice Questions based on an extract from drama/prose to test inference, evaluation and vocabulary. Any 1 out of 2 extracts to be done. **(5x1=5)**

2. Multiple Choice Questions based on an extract from poetry to test analysis and interpretation. Any 1 out of 2 extracts to be done **(5x1=5)**

Grammar **10 Marks**

Ten Multiple Choice Questions, out of twelve, to be answered. Questions shall be based on the following:

i. Tenses
ii. Modals

iii. Subject – verb concord
iv. Reported speech
   a) Commands and requests
   b) Statements
   c) Questions
v. Determiners

The following topics have been deleted for Academic Session 2020-21

A. Use of Passive Voice
B. Clauses: Noun, Adverb, Relative
C. Prepositions

PART B – Subjective Questions (40 marks)

Writing **10 Marks**

1. Formal letter (word limit 100-120 words) based on a given situation. One out of two questions is to be answered. **5 marks**

2. Writing an analytical paragraph (word limit 100-120 words) based on a given outline/ Data/ Chart/ Cue/s .One out of two questions is to be answered. **5 marks**

Literature **30 Marks**

1. **Four out of six** Short Answer Type Questions to be answered in 20-30 words each from First Flight and Footprints Without Feet (two out of three from First Flight and two out of three from Footprints Without Feet**).** **2x4=8 marks**

2. **Four out of six** Short Answer Type Questions to be answered in 40-50 words each from First Flight and Footprints Without Feet (two out of three from First Flight and two out of three from Footprints Without Feet). **3x4=12 marks**

3. **One out of two** Long Answer Type Questions from First Flight to be answered in about 100-120 words each to assess creativity, imagination and extrapolation beyond the text and across the texts. This can be a passage-based question taken from a situation/plot from the texts. **5 marks**

4. **One out of two** Long Answer Type Questions from Footprints Without Feet on theme or plot involving interpretation, extrapolation beyond the text and inference or character sketch to be answered in about 100-120 words. **5 marks**

Deleted Chapters for Academic Session 2020-21

1. FIRST FLIGHT – Text for Class X

I. How to Tell Wild Animals
II. Trees

III. Fog
IV. Mijbil the Otter
V. For Anne Gregory

2. FOOTPRINTS WITHOUT FEET – Supplementary Reader for Class X

I. The Midnight Visitor
II. A Question of Trust
III. The Book That Saved The Earth

English Prose (First Flight)

A Letter to God

1. What did Lencho hope for?

Answer: Lencho hoped for rains for his field of ripe corn. He knew that the only thing that the earth needed was a downpour or at least a shower of rain.

2. Why did Lencho say the raindrops were like 'new coins'?

Answer: A farmer knows the value of raindrops. Lencho is also a farmer. He compared the raindrops with the new coins because the raindrops would have helped him in getting a better harvest. This in turn would have brought more money. Lencho also had a good corn field. So, he hoped for some raindrops.

3. How did the rain change? What happened to Lencho's fields?

Answer: The rain was pouring as expected by Lencho. But after sometime suddenly a strong wind began to blow and along with the rain very large hailstones began to fall. These hail stones totally destroyed the corn field of Lencho. The flowers were gone from the plants. No single leaf was there on the plants.

4. What were Lencho's feelings when the hail stopped?

Answer: When the hail stopped Lencho felt very sad. After the storm was over, he stood in the middle of the corn field and said to his sons that even a plague of locusts would have left more than what was left there. He also said that they would have no corn that year and they would go hungry. It was a night of sorrow.

5. Who or what did Lencho have faith in? What did he do?

Answer: Lencho had faith in God. Lencho had the hope that God's eyes see everything, even what is deep in one's conscience. Therefore, he decided to write a letter to God. He wrote that he needed a hundred pesos so that he could sow his field again and live until the crop grew again.

6. Who read the letter?

Answer: One postman saw that the letter was addressed to God. So, he went to the post master laughing heartily and showed him the letter to God. The postmaster read the letter. He was amazed by the faith of the farmer on God.

7. What did the postmaster do then?

Answer: The postmaster tried to collect some money from his fellow workers. He himself gave a part of his salary and sent the whole money to Lencho.

8. Was Lencho surprised to find a letter for him with money in it?

Answer: No, Lencho was not surprised to find a letter for him with money in it. He had a strong belief on God. He thought that God sent the money in reply to the letter he had sent.

9. What made Lencho angry?

Answer: Lencho asked God for 100 pesos, but he received seventy pesos only. He believed that God could never make a mistake. He thought that the post office employees had stolen the rest of the amount. So, he became very angry.

10. Lencho had faith in God but lacked faith in humanity. Elaborate with reference to 'A letter to God'. (100-150 words)

Answer: Lencho had full faith in god. He lost his entire crops in the hailstorm, but he had a hope that god would help him in this time of need. He believed that no one dies of hunger. Therefore, he decided to write a letter to God. He wrote that he needed a hundred pesos so that he could sow his field again and live until the crop grew again. But when he received seventy pesos only in reply to his letter, he thought that God could never make a mistake. He believed that the post office employees had stolen the rest of the amount. He became very angry. It shows that Lencho had faith in God but he lacked faith in humanity.

Nelson Mandela: Long Walk to Freedom

1. Where did the ceremonies take place? Can you name any public buildings in India that are made of sand stone?

Answer: The ceremonies took place in the campus of the Union Building of Pretoria. In India Rashtrapati Bhawan and Red Fort are two such buildings, which are made of sand stone.

2. Can you say how 10 May is an 'autumn day' in 'South Africa'?

Answer: On 10th May 1994, many world leaders had come to the inauguration ceremony of the new democratic non racial government in South Africa. Therefore, Tenth May may be regarded as an 'autumn day' in 'South Africa'.

3. At the beginning of his speech, Mandela mentions "an extra ordinary human disaster". What does he mean by this? What is the "glorious….. human achievement" he speaks of at the end?

Answer: At the beginning of his speech Mandela mentions "an extra ordinary human disaster" to describe the cruel practice of the apartheid, i.e. the racial injustice tolerated in South Africa by the blacks at the hands of the whites. Again at the end, by the words "glorious….. human achievement", he speaks of the development of the first democratic, non-racial government in South Africa.

4. What does Mandela thank the international leaders for?

Answer: Mandela felt fortunate to be the host of the international nations since just a while ago South Africans were considered outlaws. Therefore, he thanked all the world distinguished leaders for coming to celebrate the victory of justice, peace and human dignity.

5. What ideals does he set out for the future of South Africa?

Answer: Mandela set out some ideals for the future of South Africa. He had plan to liberate the people of South Africa from the bondage of poverty, deprivation, suffering, gender and other discrimination. He also said that the beautiful land of South Africa would never again experience the oppression of one by another.

6. What do the military generals do? How has their attitude changed, and why?

Answer: The military generals of south African defence force and police saluted Mandela and pledged their loyality towards the nation. Mandela knew that they would not have done so a few years ago. Instead of that they would have arrested him. It was because of the military's loyalty to democracy. They were loyal to the new government that had been freely and fairly elected.

7. Why were two national anthems sung?

Answer: Two national anthems were sung on the day of inauguration ceremony. One was sung by the whites and the other by the blacks. This was done to show that from that day onward all the people would be treated equally.

8. How does Mandela describe the systems of government in his country (i) in the first decade, and (ii) in the final decade, of the twentieth century?

Answer:

(i) In the first decade of twentieth century, a few years after the Anglo –Boer war, the white skinned peoples of South Africa patched up their differences and erected a system of racial domination against the dark skinned peoples of their own land. The structure they created formed the basis of one of the harshest, most inhumane societies in the world.

(ii) By the final decade of the twentieth century, the system had been overturned. It was replaced by a new system, which recognized the rights and freedoms of all peoples, regardless of the colour of their skin.

9. What does courage mean to Mandela?

Answer: Mandela believed that courage is not the absence of fear, but the triumph over it. According to him, the brave man is not he who does not feel afraid, but he who conquers the fear.

10. Which does he think is natural, to love or to hate?

Answer: Mandela believed that love comes more naturally to the human heart than hate.

11. What "twin obligations" does Mandela mention?

Answer: According to Mandela, in life, every man has twin obligation. The first obligation is to his family, parents, wife and children and the second obligation is to his people, his community and his country. Each man is able to fulfill those obligations according to his own inclinations and abilities.

12. What did being free mean to Mandela as a boy, and as a student? How does he contrast these "transitory freedoms" with "the basic and honourable freedoms"?

Answer: As a boy Mandela was not hungry to be free, because he believed that he was born free. As long as he obeyed his father and abided by his tribe's traditions, he was safe in every way he knew. As a student, he wanted freedom only for himself, but all these were transitory freedoms only. As a young man he yearned for the basic and honourable freedoms of achieving his potential, earning, marrying and having a family. He felt that these freedoms were not to be obstructed in a lawful life.

13. Does Mandela think the oppressor is free? Why/ Why not?

Answer: Mandela does not think the oppressor is free, because he thinks an oppressor is a prisoner of hatred. He is locked behind the bars of prejudice and narrow-mindedness. Therefore, the oppressor must be liberated just like the oppressed.

Two Stories about Flying

I. His First Flight

1. Why was the young seagull afraid to fly? Do you think all young birds are afraid to make their First Flight, or are some birds more timid than others? Do you think a human baby also finds it a challenge to take its first steps?

Answer: The young seagull was afraid to fly, because he was frightened to see the sea below. He felt certain that his wings would never support him. No, all young birds aren't afraid to make their First Flights. Of course, some birds are more timid than others. The first attempt of anything is tough. A human baby also finds it really challenging to take its first step.

2. " The sight of the food maddened him." What does this suggest? What compelled the young seagull to finally fly?

Answer: The young seagull was very hungry. He had not eaten for a long time. When he saw his mother tearing at a piece of fish that lay at her feet he requested to get some food for him. His mother came forward but stopped midway. He was maddened by hunger and dived at the fish. He had no other option but to fly. As such the hunger compelled him to finally fly.

3. "They were beckoning to him, calling shrilly." Why did the seagull's father and mother threaten him and cajole him, to fly?

Answer: The young seagull was afraid to fly. But his brothers and his younger sister were flying happily. His parents tried to encourage him, but all went in vain. He felt that his wings would never support him. His parents threatened to let him starve on his ledge and cajoled him to fly, because the art of flying is very necessary for a bird. But he was unable to fly.

II. Black Aeroplane

1. "I'll take the risk." What is the risk? Why does the narrator take it?

Answer: The risk mentioned here is the risk of flying a small Dakota plane through the storms and black clouds. But the narrator took the risk because he wanted to reach his home and meet his family. He wanted to reach his home in England at the time of breakfast. The thought of spending time with his family made him take the risk of flying in the dark stormy clouds.

2. Describe the narrator's experience as he flew the aeroplane into the storm?

Answer: When the narrator flew into the storm, he found that everything became suddenly black. It was impossible for him to see anything outside the aeroplane. The old Dakota aeroplane jumped and twisted in the air. The compass was also not working. It was turning round and around. All other communicating devices were also dead. Suddenly, he saw another aeroplane flying next to him. The pilot signaled the narrator to follow him. With the help of the pilot of that strange black aeroplane, the narrator could land his own one at the airport. He turned to look his friend, but there was no sign of that black strange aeroplane.

3. Why does the narrator say, "I landed and was not sorry to walk away from the old Dakota….."?

Answer: The narrator experienced a horrific journey. He was delighted to come out from his old Dakota aeroplane. He wanted to know from the traffic control tower about his friend who had helped him to land safely. So, he was not sorry to walk away from the old Dakota.

4. What made the woman in the control centre look at the narrator strangely?

Answer: The narrator asked the lady in the control tower where he was and who the other pilot was. The lady found it very strange that a pilot did not know where he was. Again, there was no sign of another aircraft in the radar except the one the narrator was flying on that stormy night, so she looked at the narrator strangely.

5. Who do you think helped the narrator to reach safely? Discuss this among yourselves and give reasons for your answer.

Answer: It was none other than the narrator himself who helped him to reach safely, because, there was no other aircraft on that stormy night. Again, in a dark stormy weather flying an aeroplane without light on its wings was very strange. Therefore, the pilot must have helped himself to reach the airport. He was an efficient pilot with strong will power, so it could have been possible.

From the Diary of Anne Frank

1. What makes writing in a diary a strange experience for Anne Frank?

Answer: Anne Frank had never written anything before. She believed that nobody would be interested to read about the day to day life of a thirteen year old school girl. Therefore, she felt it to be strange to write a diary for her.

2. Why does Anne want to keep a diary?

Answer: Anne wanted to keep a diary, because she felt that she had no such friend with whom she could share her personal feelings. She heard the saying 'paper has more patience than people'. Though, she had caring parents, elder sister and numbers of friends, she felt the absence of a true friend. She needed one with whom she can share everything, but she knew that the situation would never change. Therefore, she decided to keep a diary.

3. Why did Anne think she could confide more in her diary than in people?

Answer: Anne had numbers of friends, but she did not have a true friend. She could tell them the ordinary everyday things, but she did not seem to get any closer. She accepted that it might be her fault that she could not confide in them. She knew that the situation would not change. She felt that paper has more patience than people. So, she thought she could confide more in her diary than in people.

4. Why does Anne provide a brief sketch of her life?

Answer: Anne provided a brief sketch of her life since she felt that no one would understand a word of her stories written in her diary if she were to plunge right in. Though she did not like to write about her life, she had to write a brief sketch. She treated her diary to be her best friend and called it 'Kitty'.

5. What tells you that Anne loved her grandmother?

Answer: Anne loved her grandmother very much. Her grandmother had died in January 1942. In the year she died, Anne lit a candle for her grandmother along with the rest. She expressed her grief after the death of her grandmother. She said, "No one knows how often I think of her and still love her". This shows her love towards her grandmother.

6. Why was Mr. Keesing annoyed with Anne? What did he ask her to do?

Answer: Mr. keesing was Anne's maths teacher. He was annoyed with Anne because she was a very talkative girl. After several warnings, he assigned her extra homework, asking her to write an essay on the subject, 'A chatterbox'.

7. How did Anne justify her being a chatterbox in her essay?

Answer: In her essay, Anne justified her being a chatterbox. She gave two arguments supporting herself. According to her, talking is a student's trait and she would do her best to keep it under control. She also argued that her mother was also a talkative lady. So, she had nothing to do with her inherited traits.

8. Do you think Mr. Keesing was a strict teacher?

Answer: It cannot be said that Mr. Keesing was a strict teacher, but he was a man of discipline. He was never rude to Anne. Of course, he expected the children to be silent at the class when he was teaching. He asked Anne to write an essay on 'A Chatterbox' as punishment. But, when she wrote the essay he had a good laugh. It shows that he was not so strict person.

9. What made Mr. Keesing allow Anne to talk in class?

Answer: Anne was a talkative student. Mr. Keesing asked Anne to write an essay on 'A Chatterbox' as punishment. But, Anne wrote an essay of three pages on the subject. It made him laugh. When Anne continued with her talking in the classes, she was assigned a second essay with the topic 'An Incorrigible Chatterbox'. Anne handed in the second one too. Thereafter, Mr. Keesing did not complain for two more lessons, but during the third lesson he had to punish Anne for one more time. This time the title of the essay was 'Quack, Quack, Quack, Said Mistress Chatterbox'. This time she wrote a beautiful poem with the help of her friend Sanne. Mr. Keesing read the poem to the class and in several other classes too. From then onward, she was allowed to talk in the class.

The Hundred Dresses – I

1. Where in the classroom does Wanda sit and why?

Answer: Wanda used to sit in the seat next to the last seat, in the last row in room Thirteen. She sat there because her feet were normally caked with dry mud. In order to hide her dirty feet from her classmates she used to sit in the last row.

2. Where does Wanda live? What kind of a place do you think it is?

Answer: Wanda lived in Boggins Heights. It was at a long distance from her school. It was not a developed place or a place where rich peoples lived in. The dry mud in Wanda's feet indicates that.

3. When and why do Peggy and Maddie notice Wanda's absence?

Answer: Peggy and Maddie noticed Wanda's absence on Wednesday. That day they were late for school because of Wanda. They waited for Wanda to have some fun with her but she did not come.

4. What do you think "to have fun with her" means?

Answer: Wanda was a poor girl. She used to come to school from a distant place. Her feet were normally caked with dry mud. Her classmates Peggy and Maddie made fun of her. They enjoyed the helplessness of the poor girl. This enjoyment is referred to by the term "to have fun with her".

5. In what way was Wanda different from the other children?

Answer: Wanda was different from the other children. She did not have any friend. She came to school alone. She always wore a faded blue dress that did not fit her properly. She did not talk to anybody, but a lot of girls talked to her to have a fun with her.

6. Did Wanda have a hundred dresses? Why do you think she said she did?

Answer: No, she did not have a hundred dresses. Wanda was from a very poor family. She always wore a faded blue dress. Her classmates made fun of her. To get rid of their insult she had to tell that she had a hundred of dresses.

7. Why is Maddie embarrassed by the questions Peggy asks Wanda? Is she also like Wanda, or is she different?

Answer: Maddie was embarrassed by the questions Peggy asked Wanda, because she was herself poor. She did not feel sorry for Wanda. But, she was afraid that Peggy and her classmates might insult her too for her old dresses. Peggy thought she was different from Wanda, because she would not tell them that she had a hundred dresses, if she was asked.

8. Why didn't Maddie ask Peggie to stop teasing Wanda? What was she afraid of?

Answer: Meddie didn't ask Peggy to stop teasing Wanda, because she was afraid of her. She wanted to tell Peggy by writing a note to her. As she was writing the note she pictured herself to be the next target for Peggy and other girls. So, she gave up the idea. Maddie used to wore the old dresses of Peggy. Meddie's mother tried to disguise these with new trimmings. She was afraid that Peggy might ask her where she got the dress that she had on.

9. Who did Maddie think would win the drawing contest? Why?

Answer: Maddie thought that Peggy would win the drawing contest, because she could copy a picture in a magazine or some film star's head so perfectly that one could almost tell who it was.

10. Who won the drawing contest? What had the winner drawn?

Answer: Wanda Petronski won the drawing contest for the girls. She drew one hundred designs of dresses. All were different in colours and they were beautiful. The judges were of the opinion that any one of the drawings is worthy of winning the prize.

The Hundred Dresses – II

1. What did Mr Petronski's letter say?

Answer: Mr. Petronski in his letter said that Wanda and Jake would not come to school anymore as they were moving to a big city. He also said that in that new city nobody would ask them why their names were so funny. Nobody would call them 'Pollack' there.

2. Is Miss Mason angry with the class, or is she unhappy and upset?

Answer: Rather than being angry, Miss Mason was unhappy and upset with the class. She thought that the behaviour of the students towards Wanda was very unfortunate. She believed that they had not insulted her purposefully. But this was a very unfortunate and sad thing to happen.

3. How does Maddie feel after listening to the note from Wanda's father?

Answer: After listening to the note from Wanda's father, Maddie had a very sick feeling. She could not put her mind on her lessons. She felt what Peggy had done was bad, but she stood by her. It was worse. She thought herself to be coward. Maddie hadn't considered her act to be wrong, but, she knew that they were wrong.

4. What does Maddie want to do?

Answer: Maddie wanted to tell wanda that she had not meant to hurt her feelings. She hoped that Peggy would accompany her to Boggins Height. She might not have moved away. They would tell Wanda that she had won the drawing contest. She would also tell her that she was smart and the dresses were beautiful.

5. What excuses does Peggy think up for her behaviour? Why?

Answer: Peggy thought up an excuse for her behaviour. She never called Wanda a foreigner or made fun of her long name. She proposed Maddie to go to Boggins Height to see if Wanda had left the town or not. She never thought Wanda had the sense to know that they were making fun of her. She assumed Wanda to be a dumb girl. Peggy made these excuses because she felt guilty for her act.

6. What are Maddie's thoughts as they go to Boggins Hieghts?

Answer: Maddie hoped that they would find Wanda. She wanted to tell Wanda that they were sorry for their behaviour towards her. She also wanted to tell her how wonderful the whole school thought she was. She would request her not to move away and everybody would be nice. Maddie would tell her that both of them would fight anybody who was not nice.

7. Why does Wanda's house remind Maddie of Wanda's blue dress?

Answer: Wanda's house was shabby but clean. It reminded Maddie of Wanda's faded blue cotton dress, because it was also shabby but clean.

8. What does Maddie think hard about? What important decision does she come to?

Answer: Peggy and Maddie could not find Wanda. Maddie could not sleep that night. She thought about Wanda, her faded blue dress and her little shabby but clean house. She thought hard about the wonderful exhibition of hundred dresses drawn by Wanda. At last she came to the conclusion that she would never stand by and say nothing again. If she ever heard anybody picking on someone because they were funny looking or because they had strange names, she would protest. She would never make anybody unhappy again.

9. What did the girls write to Wanda?

Answer: The girls wrote a friendly letter to Wanda telling about the contest. In the letter they told Wanda that she had won the contest. They wrote how pretty her drawings were. They asked Wanda if she liked where she was living and if she liked her new teacher. They signed the letter with lots of X's for love.

10. Did they get a reply? Who was more anxious for a reply, Peggy or Maddie? How do you know?

Answer: They did not get any reply for their letter from Wanda. Maddie thought that Wanda might be hurt and angry. Maddie was more anxious for a reply. Peggy had begun to forget the whole business, but maddie could not. She put herself to sleep at night making speeches about Wanda, defending her from great crowds of girls who were trying to insult her for her dresses. This shows that she was more anxious for the reply from poor Wanda.

11. How did the girls know that Wanda liked them even though they had teased her?

Answer: The girls know that Wanda liked them even though they had teased her, because she had asked Miss Mason to give the Green dress to Peggy and the blue one to Maddie. Peggy and Maddie brought home the two dresses. When Maddie looked carefully the drawing of the blue dress, she found that the girl in the drawing was none other than Maddie. She ran over to Peggy's house. They found that the girl in green dress was Peggy only. Now, they could realize that Wanda liked them though they had teased her.

Glimpses of India

I. A Baker from Goa

1. What are the elders in Goa nostalgic about?

Answer: The elders in Goa were nostalgic about the good old Portuguese days, the Portuguese and their famous loaves of bread.

2. Is bread-making still popular in Goa? How do you know?

Answer: Yes, bread making is still popular in Goa. Now also, there are the mixtures, the moulders and the bakers who bake the loaves. The age old furnaces still exist there in Goa. The thud and jingle of the traditional baker's bamboo, announcing his arrival in the morning can still be heard in some places.

3. What is the baker called?

Answer: The bakers in Goa are called pader.

4. When would the baker come every day? Why did the children run to meet him?

Answer: The baker used to come at least twice a day. Once, when he set out in the morning on his selling round, and then again, when he returned after emptying his huge basket. The children ran to meet the baker for the bread bangles, which they chose carefully. Sometimes, it was a sweet bread of special make.

5. What did the bakers wear: (i) in the Portuguese days? (ii) When the author was young?

Answer: (i) In the Portuguese days, the baker or bread-seller used to wear a peculiar dress known as the kabai. It was a single piece long frock reaching down to the knees.

(ii) When the author was young, bakers wore a shirt and trousers which were shorter than full length ones and longer than half pants.

6. Who invites the comment-"he is dressed like a pader"? Why?

Answer: Anyone who wears a half pant which reaches just below the knees invites the comment that he is dressed like a pader. It is because the bakers in Goa who are called pader wear trousers shorter than full length ones and longer than half pants.

7. Where were the monthly accounts of the baker recorded?

Answer: The bakers usually collected their money at the end of the month. The monthly accounts used to be recorded on some wall in pencil.

8. What does a 'jackfruit-like appearance' mean?

Answer: A 'jackfruit like appearance' means a plump physique. Baking was a profitable business in the old days. The baker and his family never starved. The baker, his family or servants always looked happy. They were of plump physiques. To describe such a physique 'jackfruit like appearance' is used.

9. How is bread an important part of life in Goa? Explain in 30-40 words.

Answer: In Goa, marriage gifts are meaningless without the sweet bread known as thebol. Cakes and bolinhas are a must for Christmas as well as other festivals. The lady of the house must prepare sandwiches on the occasion of her daughter's marriage ceremony. Therefore, bread is an important part of life in Goa.

II. Coorg

1. Where is Coorg?

Answer: Coorg or Kodagu is the smallest district of Karnataka.

2. What is the story about the Kodavu people's descent?

Answer: There is a story that a part of Alexander's army moved south along the coast and settled in Coorg, because it was impossible for them to return to their own land. These people married amongst the locals and their culture is apparent in the marital traditions. Their religious rites are distinct from the mainstream Hindus.

III. Tea from Assam

1. Describe the Indian legend about the discovery of tea.

Answer: The Indian legend about the tea is related to Bodhidharma an ancient Boddhist ascetic. Bodhidharma cut off his eyelids because he felt sleepy during meditation. Ten tea plants grew out of these eyelids and when the leaves of these plants were put in hot water and drank that banished his sleep.

2. Describe the scene of both the sides of the gravel road.

Answer: On the both sides of the gravel road there were acre upon acre of tea bushes, all are neatly pruned to the same height. Groups of tea-pluckers wearing plastic apron and bamboo baskets on their back were plucking newly sprouted tea leaves.

3. What did Rajvir tell Pranjol about tea?

Answer: Rajvir told Pranjol that over eighty crore cups of tea are drunk every day throughout the world. He told Pranjol two legends related to the discovery of tea. He told him that tea was first drunk in China as far back as 2700 BC. Tea came to Europe only in the sixteenth century and was drunk more as medicine than beverages. He also told Pranjol that the second flush or sprouting period, that is from May to July, yields the best tea.

4. Describe the magnificent view of tea gardens seen by Rajvir on his way?

Answer: Rajvir saw a sea of tea bushes stretched as far as the eye could see against the backdrop of densely wooded hills. Dwarfing the tiny tea plants were tall and sturdy shade trees. And in the midst of orderly rows of tea bushes they busily moved their doll like figures. It was a magnificent view.

5. Why did Pranjol's father say that Rajvir had done his homework before visiting Assam?

Answer: Rajvir was excited about visiting tea garden and thus, he studied a lot about the tea industry before visiting Assam and shared his knowledge. He knew a lot about the tea gardens. Thus, Pranjol's father said that Rajvir had already done his homework before visiting Assam.

6. In what ways is China related to tea?

Answer: Tea was first drunk in China. It was about 2700 B.C. In fact, the words 'chai' and 'chini' are Chinese words. There is a legend about the discovery of tea. A Chinese emperor used to drink boiled water and one day a few leaves of the twigs burning under the pot fell into the boiled water. The water became delicious in flavor. It is believed that these were tea leaves.

Madam Rides the Bus

1. What was Valli's favourite pastime?

Answer: Valli's favourite pastime was standing in the front doorway of her house, watching what was happening in the street outside.

2. What was a source of unending joy for Valli? What was her strongest desire?

Answer: The most fascinating thing for Valli was the bus that travelled between her village and the nearest town. The sight of the bus, filled each time with a new set of passengers was a source of unending joy for Valli. Valli's strongest desire was to ride on the bus and go to the town.

3. What did Valli find out about the bus journey? How did she find out these details?

Answer: Valli could find out that the town was six miles away from the village. The bus fare to the town was thirty paise one way and it took forty five minutes of travelling time. She gathered these information from the conversations between her neighbours and people who regularly used the bus. She also asked a few discreet questions here and there.

4. What do you think Valli was planning to do?

Answer: Valli was planning to go to the town at least for once. She would ride the bus and after reaching the town she would come back home on the same bus. For the purpose, she collected information like bus fare, travelling time, distance etc.

5. Why does the conductor call Valli 'madam'?

Answer: When the conductor stretched out his hand to help Valli to get on the bus, she said that she could get on by herself and she did not require the help of the conductor. Her act was of a grown up girl and therefore the conductor called her 'madam'.

6. Why does Valli stand up on the seat? What does she see now?

Answer: Valli stood up on her seat, because her view was cut off by a canvass blind that covered the lower part of her window. She saw that the road was very narrow, on one side of which there was a canal and beyond it, there were palm trees, grassland, distant mountains and the blue sky. On the other side, there was a deep ditch and many acres of green fields as far as one could see.

7. What does Valli tell the elderly man when he calls her a child?

Answer: When the elderly man called her a child Valli told that there was nobody on the bus who was a child. She had paid her full fare of thirty paise like everyone else.

8. Why didn't Valli want to make friends with the elderly woman?

Answer: Valli did not like to make friends with the elderly woman, because she was not attractive at all. She was wearing ugly earrings in the big holes in her earlobes. She was chewing beetle nut and the beetle juice was about to spill over her lips at any time. Valli did not find her to be a lady with whom she could be sociable with.

9. How did Valli save up money for her first journey? Was it easy for her?

Answer: Valli had saved the money for her first bus journey resolutely resisting her strong urges to buy peppermints, toys, balloons etc. It was difficult on her part to resist herself from riding the merry-go-round at the village fair. But, she was determined to save sixty paise and thriftily saved whatever stray coins came her way.

10. What did Valli see on her way that made her laugh?

Answer: Valli saw a young cow with his tail high in the air, was running very fast right in the middle of the road. He was in front of the bus. The bus driver sounded his horn loudly, but the frightened cow was running faster right in front of the bus. Valli found the scene very funny and laughed until there were tears in her eyes.

11. Why didn't she get off the bus at the bus station?

Answer: Valli did not want to get off the bus as she was afraid to do so. Another reason was that she had not enough money to buy something at the bus station too. She just wanted to have a bus ride and return to her home.

12. Why didn't Valli want to go to the stall and have a drink? What does this tell you about her?

Answer: Valli did not have enough money to buy something to drink. That is why she did not get off the bus and go to the stall. Though the bus conductor offered her a cold drink, she refused it. It shows that she was a determined girl and her only desire was to ride the bus. She was a girl of self respect and did not like to take the help of others.

13. What was Valli's deepest desire? Find the words and phrases in the story that tell you this.

Answer: Valli's deepest desire was to ride the bus that travelled between her village and the nearest town. The sentence in the story which tells us about her desire to go to the town by riding the bus is "Day after day she watched the bus, and gradually a tiny wish crept into her head and grew there: she wanted to ride on that bus, even if just once."

14. Valli shows extraordinary courage in taking a bus journey all alone. Explain how ability and courage are essential to fulfill one's dream. (100-150 words)

Answer: We cannot deny the fact that ability and courage are essential to fulfill one's dream. Valli shows extraordinary courage in taking a bus journey all alone. She planned the journey for long time. For the purpose the little girl gathered information from different sources. She saved money for the purpose resolutely resisting her strong urges to buy peppermints, toys, balloons, fun ride etc. She was determined to save sixty paise and thriftily saved whatever stray coins came her way. Though she had never gone to the town, she had the courage to travel all alone. She enjoyed the ride. She did not buy anything in the bus station. She did not get off the bus too. All these show her determination, ability and courage to fulfill the dream to ride the bus.

The Sermon at Benares

1. When her son dies, Kisa Gotami goes from house to house. What does she ask for? Does she get it? Why not?

Answer: When Kisa Gotami lost her son, she went from house to house carrying her dead son. She asked for medicine from her neighbours for her dead son. She did not get the medicine, because no medicine can make a dead man alive. They thought that Kisa Gotami had lost her senses.

2. Kisa Gotami again goes from house to house after she speaks with the Buddha. What does she ask for, the second time around? Does she get it? Why not?

Answer: When Kisa Gotami visited the Buddha and told about her dead son, Buddha asked her to bring a handful of mustard seeds from a house where no one had lost a child, husband, parent or friend. Kisa Gotami went from house to house to collect the mustard seeds, but she did not get such a house. In every house, some beloved one had died in it.

3. What does Kisa Gotami understand the second time that she failed to understand the first time? Was this what the Buddha wanted her to understand?

Answer: At the second time, Kisa Gotami could understand that she was not alone who had lost her beloved one. At the first time she was in such a grief that she had become selfish and could not understand the fact. This was exactly what the Buddha wanted Kisa Gotami to understand.

4. Why do you think Kisa Gotami understood this only the second time? In what way did the Buddha change her understanding?

Answer: Kisa Gotami could understand that death is common to all the second time only. Earlier, she was very selfish for the grief of her lost son. So, she could not understand it. When the Buddha asked her to collect a handful of mustard seeds from a house where no one had died, she could not get it. As such she could understand that nobody can avoid dying.

5. How do you usually understand the idea of 'selfishness'? Do you agree with Kisa Gotami that she was being 'selfish in her grief'?

Answer: Selfishness means our tendency to think for ourselves only. A selfish man cannot understand the facts of life. Yes, Kisa Gotami was being 'selfish in her grief'. That is why she could not feel the grief of others. She thought her to be alone who had lost her beloved one.

Buddha made her understand that a soul can be free from the deepest pain of life if he can surrender his selfishness.

6. Life is full of trials and tribulations which can be overcome by a human being through his own efforts. Explain with reference to Kisa Gotami's life. (100-150 words)

Answer: Life is full of trials and tribulations which can be overcome by a human being through his own efforts. Kisa Gotami had an only son. When her child died, Kisa Gotami went from house to house carrying her dead son. She asked for medicine from her neighbours for her dead son. She did not accept the truth that her child is dead. She did not get the medicine. People thought that Kisa Gotami had lost her senses. She went to Lord Buddha. He asked her to bring a handful of mustard seeds from the house where no one has died ever. Kisa Gotami could not find a single such house. She could understand that death is common to all. If we do not accept this truth we will be in great pain. Of course, there is a path that leads to mental peace and happiness to those who surrender all selfishness.

The Proposal

1. What does Chubukov at first suspect that Lomov has come for? Is he sincere when he later says "And I've always loved you, my angel, as if you were my own son"? Find reasons for your answer from the play.

Answer: At the beginning Chubukov suspects that Lomov has come to borrow money from Chubukov. He is not sincere when he later says "And I've always loved you, my angel, as if you were my own son". It is very much clear from his behaviour towards Lomov from the very beginning. He is not very happy to see Lomov in his house in evening dress. He becomes cheerful only when he comes to know that he has come with a marriage proposal for Natalya. In front of Natalya he calls Lomov a merchant. Later on, they quarrel over the Oxen Meadows. It means that Chubukov does not like Lomov.

2. How does Lomov come to Chubukov's house? What for does he come? How is he received?

Answer: Lomov came to Chubukov's house in the evening dress with gloves on. He came to ask the hand of chubukov's daughter Natalya. He was received with all the respect by Chubukov.

3. How does Chubukov react when Lomov says that he has come to ask for the hand of his daughter?

Answer: When Lomov says that he has come to ask for the hand of his daughter, Chubukov gets off balanced with joy. He embraces and kisses Lomov, sheds a tear of joy and calls for god's blessing for Lomov and Natalya.

English Poetry (First Flight)

Dust of Snow

1. What is a "dust of snow"? What does the poet say has changed his mood? How has the poet's mood changed?

Answer: The 'dust of snow' means the flakes of snow. The dust of snow showers all of a sudden, which changed the poet's mood. The poet feels better, the sadness disappears and he gets refreshed after the showering of snowy flakes. He remains happy for the rest of the day.

2. How does Frost present nature in this poem? The following questions may help you to think of an answer.

(i) What are the birds that are usually named in poems? Do you think a crow is often mentioned in poems? What images come to your mind when you think of a crow?

(ii) Again what is "a hemlock tree"? Why doesn't the poet write about a more 'beautiful' tree such as a maple, or an oak, or a pine?

(iii) What do the 'crow' and 'hemlock' represent- joy or sorrow? What does the dust of snow that the crow shakes off a hemlock tree stand for.

Answer: Frost presents nature in an extra ordinary manner in the poem.

i) Usually, poets mentions the birds and trees which are known for their beauty and good qualities, like cuckoo, peacock etc. and trees full of beautiful flowers like oak, maple etc. But, here Frost brings a new approach. He mentions a crow. Crow is an ugly bird which is not often used in poems. When we think of a crow, it brings a picture of sadness and hopelessness to our mind.

ii) A hemlock tree is a poisonous plant with small white flowers. The poet, Robert Frost, has not written about an oak, maple or pine tree. Instead of those, he chooses the hemlock. It is felt that the poet did so to symbolise his state of mind, the sorrow and grief.

iii) The crow and hemlock tree represent sorrow and depression. The dust of snow is the symbol of joy. The dust of snow that the crow shakes off a hemlock tree symbolically means experiencing the feelings of joy and enthusiasm leaving aside the heavy loads of depression and grief.

Fire and Ice

1. There are many ideas about how the world will 'end'. Do you think the world will end some day? Have you ever thought what would happen if the sun got so hot that it 'burst' or grew colder?

Answer: Though it is unfortunate, but we must accept that the world is going to end one day and there is nothing we can do about it. There are many ideas as to how it will end but nothing is commonly accepted theory. If the sun gets so hot one day that it bursts, it would destroy the whole world as everything would be burnt. On the other hand, if it grows colder, there would be no life, because without the solar energy nothing can survive in the world. The reason that life exists only on Earth is that the circumstances and temperature is very much favourable for the animals as well as the plants in the earth.

2. For Frost, what do 'fire' and 'ice' stand for? Here are some ideas

greed	**avarice**	**cruelty**	**lust**
conflict	**fury**	**intolerance**	**rigidity**
insensitivity	**coldness**	**indifference**	**hatred**

Answer: For the poet 'Frost' 'fire' stands for greed, avarice, lust, conflict and fury. 'Ice' stands for cruelty, intolerance, rigidity, insensitivity, coldness, indifference and hatred.

3. Some say the world will end in fire
Some say in ice
From that I have tasted of desire
I hold with those who favour fire"

- **i. Name the poem and the poet**
- **ii. What are the two destructive forces?**
- **iii. What do they stand for?**
- **iv. What does he favour**

Answer:

i. These lines are quoted from the poem 'Fire and Ice' by the poet Robert Frost.
ii. 'Fire' and 'Ice' are the two destructive forces according to the poet.
iii. 'Fire' stands for desire, greed etc. and 'Ice' stands for rigidity, hatred etc.
iv. The poet Robert Frost favours a society free from 'Fire' and 'Ice'. It means that the negative forces like greediness, rigidity, Furiousness etc should be eliminated from the human society; otherwise the mankind will be banished one day.

A Tiger in the Zoo

1. **"He should be lurking in shadow,**
Sliding through long grass
Near the water hole
Where plump deer pass."

a. **The poem, "a Tiger in the Zoo" is written by**
   (i) Leslie Norris (ii) William Blake
   (iii) Peter Niblett (iv) Robert Frost

b. **The tiger should be lurking in the shadow**
   (i) for his prey (ii) for taking rest
   (iii) for leisure (iv) for scaring others

c. **The deer frequents the water hole to ____________________**

d. **The phrase 'lurking in the shadow' here means____________**

Answer:

a. The poem, "a Tiger in the Zoo" is written by (i) Leslie Norris
b. The tiger should be lurking in the shadow (i) for his prey
c. The deer frequents the water hole to drink water.
d. The phrase 'lurking in the shadow' here means the act of waiting for prey hiding in the long grass by the tiger.

2. **Describe some of the activities of the tiger at zoo as stated by the poet.?**

Answer: Some of the activities of the tiger as stated by the poet are – walking along the cage, ignoring the visitors, hearing the sounds of patrolling of cars and staring at the stars of the sky.

3. **What does the poet want to convey through the poem?**

Answer: The poet tries to exhibit the miserable life of a caged tiger in the zoo. He puts before us the two different pictures of life, i.e., in the zoo and the natural life under the open sky. According to the poet, animals should not be caged. They have the right to live freely in the jungle. We cage them only for our entertainment and to enjoy their miserable state of life, which is not correct.

4. **Do you agree that wild animals should be caged? Comment 'yes' or 'no' giving reasons.**

Answer: Wild animals should not be caged. Caging wild animal is against the rules of natural justice. Earlier the wild animals used to move around the forest freely, but now they are kept in the zoo just to entertain the visitors. This is a cruel act. A tiger who rules over a large forest is confined in a small cage. Thereby we snatched the right to live a free life from them. They forget the art of hunting or terrorising the people. Therefore they should not be caged.

5. **Why does the tiger express his anger quietly?**

Answer: The tiger expresses his anger quietly, because he is helpless. He can do nothing as he is caged under steel bars. The tiger is locked in a concrete cell, so he cannot punish those who have snatched his right to live freely. The tiger can only show his anger.

The Ball Poem

1. Why does the poet say, "I would not intrude on him"? Why does not he offer him money to buy another ball?

Answer : The poet says, "I would not intrude on him", because he wants the boy to understand the meaning of loss of his own goods. He does not buy a new ball for him as he feels it to be a good lesson that everyone should know. A new ball is worthless, but the sense of responsibility and the grief of losing own good is very important in the boy's life.

2. "....staring down

All his young days into the harbor where

His ball went...

Do you think the boy has had the ball for a long time?

Answer: Yes, it seems that the boy has had the ball for a long time. When he lost his ball, all his memories of childhood days flashed back to his mind. Another ball was worthless for him as he could not get back his childhood days.

3. What does " in the world of possessions" mean?

Answer: In the poem 'The Ball Poem', the line "in the world of possessions" means the world where everybody is busy in the race to posses more and more. The poet wants to make the boy understand that money is external. One can buy the material things out of money but not the memories with the lost assets.

4. What does the poet say the boy is learning from the loss of the ball? Try to explain this in your own words.

Answer: The poet says that the boy is learning to accept the loss. He learns that a man loses many things in life and the memories attached with are very difficult to get back in future. He also learns the value of possession and the sense of responsibility after losing his ball which he claimed to be his own. The boy was in grief because he could understand that some of the moments are really invaluable in life.

Amanda

1. How old do you think Amanda is? How do you know this?

Answer: As described in the poem Amanda is a teenager school going girl. We can understand that from some of the advices and instructions given to Amanda. Amanda is asked to complete her homework and to clean her shoes. She is warned not to eat chocolates as she has acne. This shows that she is an adolescent girl.

2. Who do you think is speaking to Amanda?

Answer: It seems that one of the parents is speaking to Amanda. It may be her mother as the girl children are taken care of at home more by their mother, but the same is not confirmed.

3. What could Amanda do if she were a mermaid?

Answer: Amanda wants to be a mermaid and to become the sole inhabitant of the beautiful sea. Amanda could swim lazily enjoying the waves if she were a mermaid.

4. Is Amanda an orphan? Why does she say so?

Answer: No, Amanda is not an orphan child as she is advised and warned constantly by one of her parents in the poem. She wished if she were an orphan as the orphans have nobody to warn and to resist against doing something which they like.

Animals

1. Notice the use of the word 'turn' in the first line, "I think I could turn and live with animals….". What is the poet turning from?

Answer: In the first line of the poem 'Animal' the poet mentions the word 'turn'. The poet wants to turn from human being to animal and to live with them as he finds humans complicated and false. He likes the animals as they are self contained and they never complain for what they are not getting.

2. Mention three things that humans do and animals don't.

Answer: Animals do not cry for their conditions, but human beings do. All the animals are well satisfied with their belongings. They are not in a race to own the material things like the human beings. Humans commit sins and weep at the dark, but the animals need not to weep as they have no confession.

The Tale of Custard the Dragon

1. Who are the characters in this poem? List them with their pet names.

Answer: The characters in the poem 'The Tale of Custard the Dragon' are Belinda, a black kitten, a little grey mouse, a little yellow dog, a dragon and a pirate. The pet names of the pet characters are-

Characters	**Pet names**
Kitten	Ink
Mouse	Blink
Dog	Mustard
Dragon	Custard

2. Why did Custard cry for a nice safe cage? Why is the dragon called "cowardly dragon"?

Answer: Custard cried for a nice safe cage, because it was a coward dragon. The dragon was called a "cowardly dragon" as the other members in the house were brave. Belinda was as brave as a barrel full of bears, Ink and Blink chased lions and Mustard is as brave as an angry tiger. Therefore, they thought Custard a coward one.

3. "Belinda tickled him, she tickled him unmerciful…." why?

Or

Why did Belinda tickle the dragon?

Answer: Belinda tickled the dragon unmercifully, because he was coward and he cried for a safe cage. Belinda , Ink, Blink and Mustard laughed at the dragon for his cowardice act.

Supplementary Reader (Footprints Without Feet)

A Triumph of Surgery

1. Why is Mrs. Pumphrey worried about Tricki?

Answer: Mrs Pumphrey is worried about Tricki, because she believes that Tricki is very weak. She thinks that Tricki is suffering from malnutrition.

2. What does she do to help him? Is she wise in this?

Answer: Mrs. Pumphrey gives Tricki malt, cod-liver oil, Horlicks etc. apart from his normal diet. She gives Tricki cream cakes and chocolates too as she feels him to be very weak. She cannot be said to be wise in this.

3. Who does 'I' refer to in the story 'A triumph of surgery'?

Answer: In the story 'A triumph of surgery', 'I' refers to Mr. Herriot, a veterinary surgeon.

4. Is the narrator of the story 'A triumph of surgery' as rich as Tricki's mistress?

Answer: The narrator of the story 'A triumph of surgery' is not as rich as Tricki's mistress. Mrs. Pumphrey is richer in comparison to Mr. Herriot.

5. How does he treat the dog?

Answer: Mr. Herriot knows that the cause of Tricki's illness is nothing but over eating and lack of exercises. Therefore, the veterinary surgeon keeps him hungry for two days and gives only plenty of water to drink. From third day onward he showed some interest in food. He starts to play with the other dogs. He becomes a lithe, hard-muscled dog in just a fortnight.

6. Why is he tempted to keep Tricki on as a permanent guest?

Answer: Mrs. Pumphrey brings dozen of eggs and bottles of wines for Tricki to build up his strength. Mr. Herriot and his partners consume the eggs and wine. These are the days of contentment for them. She also brings Brandy. He knows that these types of rich foods are not good for Tricki. But Mr. Herriot becomes very happy having these costly foods. He is tempted to keep Tricki on as a permanent guest.

7. Why does Mrs. Pumphrey think the dog's recovery is "a triumph of surgery"?

Answer: Mrs. Pumphrey thinks the dog's recovery to be "a triumph of surgery", because she does not know that the reason of Tricki's illness is nothing but her excessive care. She believes that the dog's recovery has become possible only because of his treatment in the surgery.

The Thief's Story

1. **Who does 'I' refer to in the story 'The Thief's Story'?**

Answer:

In the writing 'The Thief's Story', 'I' refers to the thief.

2. **What is the story teller "a fairly successful hand" at?**

Answer:

The story teller is a fairly successful hand at theft.

3. **What does he get from Anil in return for his work?**

Answer:

The Thief does not get any monthly salary from Anil for his work. He makes some profit out of daily marketing.

4. **How does the thief think Anil will react to the theft?**

Answer: The thief feels that there will be a touch of sadness in the face of Anil when he will discover the theft.

5. **What does he say about the different reactions of people when they are robbed?**

Answer:

The thief remarks that the reactions of different people are different when they are robbed. The greedy man shows fear, the rich man shows anger, the poor man shows acceptance, but a simple and kind hearted person like Anil becomes sad for the loss of trust.

6. **Does Anil realise that he has been robbed?**

Answer:

Anil knows that he has been robbed. But he does not express the same.

Footprints Without Feet

1. How did the invisible man first become visible?

Answer: The invisible scientist, Griffin first became visible when his muddy footprints were noticed by two boys on the steps of a house in London.

Answer: Griffin, the scientist was a lawless person. His landlord did not like him. He tried to eject him. Griffin set fire to the house to take revenge on the owner. He removed all of his clothes, so that he could get away without being seen. Thereafter, he became a homeless wanderer without clothes and used to wandering in the streets.

3. Why does Mrs. Hall find the scientist eccentric?

Answer: Mrs. Hall found the scientist eccentric because of his strange behaviour. She tried to talk in a friendly way but he had no desire to talk. He said that he had come there for solitude and did not wish to be disturbed in his work.

4. What curious episode occurs in the study?

Answer: On a very early morning, a clergyman and his wife were awakened by noises in their study. When they were coming downstairs, they heard the sound of coins being taken from the clergyman's desk. However, to their amazement they did not find anybody there in the study when they entered the room. Yet the desk had been opened and the house keeping money was missing. This made them curious.

5. What other extra ordinary things happen at the inn?

Answer: At the Inn, Mrs.Hall and her husband found the door of the scientist's room wide open. They did not want to miss the chance and entered the room. But the scientist was not seen in the room. Mrs. Hall heard the sniffing sound of somebody and the hat on the bedpost leapt up and dashed into her face. Then the bedroom chair sprang up into the air and pushed them both out of the room. This made Mrs. Hall convinced that the room was haunted by some spirits and the scientist was responsible for all these extra ordinary things to happen.

The Making of a Scientist

1. How did a book become a turning point in Richard Ebright's life?

Answer: Richard Elbright's mother got him a children's book called 'The Travels of Monach X', which told how monarch butterflies migrate to Central America. This book became a turning point in Richard Elbright's life. He was already interested in collecting butterflies. By the time he was in the second grade, he had collected all the twenty five species of butterflies found around his hometown. The new book aroused his interest in Monarch butterflies and opened the world of science to him. He began to raise monarch butterflies at the basement of his home and studied them in different stages of their development.

2. How did his mother help him?

Answer: Richard Elbright's mother helped him by encouraging his interest in learning. She was a good friend of him. She used to get him instruments like telescopes, microscopes, cameras mounting materials and other equipments. His mother took him on trips to meet his curiosity.

3. What lesson does Ebright learn when he does not win anything at a scientific fair?

Answer: When Elbright did not win anything at the science fair, he realised that the winners had tried to conduct real experiments. They did not simply make a neat display.

4. What experiments and projects does he then undertake?

Answer: Richard Elbright undertook a project of finding the cause of a viral disease that killed nearly all monarch caterpillars every few years. He thought that the disease might have been carried by a beetle. So, he tried to raise caterpillars in the presence of beetles. Though he did not get any real result, he showed that he had tried and won a prize this time.

5. What are the qualities that go into the making of a scientist?

Answer: The author has mentioned three qualities that go into the making of a scientist. Those are- a fast-rate mind, curiosity and the will to win for the right reason. Richard Elbright was a good speaker, a champion debater and a good canoeist. He was an expert photographer, particularly of nature and scientific exhibits. His all-around interest and never ending curiosity made him a good scientist.

The Necklace

1. What kind of a person is Mme loisel - why is she always unhappy?

Answer: Mme Loisel is from a poor family. She feels her poverty to be a curse upon her. She is very pretty girl. She thinks she is born to enjoy all the luxuries of life. But her husband is a petty clerk and they don't have good apartment to stay in and nice dresses to wear. As such she always remains unhappy.

2. What kind of a person is her husband?

Answer: Mme Loisel's husband is a very simple and kind hearted fellow. He is a petty clerk but he always tries to make Mme Loisel happy. He buys a new dress for her with all his savings. Again, when she loses the borrowed necklace, he spends the entire money his father left him. He borrows the rest to replace the necklace. It shows his love towards his wife.

3. What fresh problem now disturbs Mme Loisel?

Answer: The fresh problem that disturbs Mme Loisel after getting the new dress is that she does not have any good jewelry to wear. This makes her sad.

4. How is the problem solved?

Answer: Mme Loisel's husband asked her to request her friend Mme Forestier to lend her some jewels. Mme Loisel found the idea good and approached Mme Forestier. She lent a necklace which Mme Loisel found the most beautiful. In this way the problem of jewel was solved.

5. What do M. and Mme Loisel do next?

Answer: When M. and Mme Loisel discovered that the necklace was missing they tried to find out where it could have been lost. They thought that it could have been dropped in the cab. But they did not know the number of the cab. Mr. Loisel searched the track where they walked, but could not find the necklace. They went to the police and to the cab offices. He put an advertisement in the newspapers offering a reward. At last, Matilda wrote a letter to Mme Forestier explaining that she had broken the clasp of the necklace and would have it repaired. Then they decided to replace the lost necklace with a new one.

6. How do they replace the necklace?

Answer: Mr. Loisel had no other option but to purchase a new one. They had to pay thirty six thousand francs for it. Mr. Loisel had Eighteen thousand francs he had received from his father. He borrowed the rest and bought the diamond necklace.

The Hack Driver

1. Why is the lawyer sent to New Mullion? What does he first think about the place?

Answer: The lawyer is sent to New Mullion to serve summons on a man called Oliver Lutkins. He thinks that New Mullion will be a sweet and simple country village.

2. Who befriends him? Where does he take him?

Answer: A hack driver befriends him. He offers to help the lawyer. He takes him to all the places where Oliver Lutkins can be found. Initially, they go to Fritz's shop. Then they go to Gustaff's barber shop and Gray's barber shop. Thereafter, they go to the pool room. At last, he is taken to the farm of Lutkin's mother.

3. What does he say about Lutkins?

Answer: The hack driver says that Oliver Lutkins is not easy to catch. Lutkins owes money to many people. But he never pays anybody a cent. Again he says that Lutkins is not really bad, but it is hard to make him part with his money.

4. What more does Bill say about Lutkins and his family?

Answer: Bill, the hack driver told that Lutkins mother was a terror. She was about nine feet tall and four feet thick. She had a farm at a distance of three miles from the town. Lutkins might have escaped and taken shelter at the firm.

5. Does the narrator serve the summons that day?

Answer: No, the narrator does not serve the summons that day. Bill, the fake hack driver makes him a fool. He offers to help him to find Lutkins. The lawyer accepts the offer, but the whole day, Lutkins in disguise of Bill misguides the lawyer and takes him to different places.

6. Who is Lutkins?

Answer: Lutkins is a hack driver. He lives in New Mullion. He is a very clever person. Lutkins is a witness in a law case. He was about forty years of age and a cheerful person. He fools the lawyer all day long and takes him to different places.

7. **"I agreed that it was pretty disrespectful treatment. We did, however, search the house. Since it was only one story high, Bill went round it, peering in at all the windows. We examined the barn and stable."**

a. **Who does 'I' refer to-**

(i) Sinclair lewis **(ii) Carol Lewis**

(iii) Oliver lutkins **(iv) Leslie Norris**

b. **What was Bill's profession?**

(i) Lawyer **(ii) hack driver**

(iii) guide **(iv) drama artist**

c. **The disrespectful treatment faced by the speaker was_______________**

d. **The phrase 'peering in at all windows' here means________________**

Answer: (a) (i) Sinclair lewis

(b) (ii) hack driver

(c) the behaviour of Oliver Lutkin's mother, who shouted at them, threatened them and drove them away.

(d) to look inside

Bholi

1. Why is Bholi's father worried about her?

Answer: Bholi's father is worried about her marriage, because she is neither beautiful nor intelligent. Nobody will come forward with a marriage proposal.

2. For what unusual reasons is Bholi sent to school?

Answer: The Tehsildar urges Ramlal to send his daughters to the newly opened school. He wants him to set an example for others. Ramlal discusses the matter with his wife, but she is against sending girls to school. She thinks nobody marries girls who have been to school. But there is a little chance of Bholi getting married. She is neither good looking nor intelligent. So, they decide to send her to school.

3. Does Bholi enjoy her first day at school?

Answer: Yes, Bholi enjoys her first day at school. She feels happy to get so many girls of her age at school. She hopes that one of these girls may become her friend. The teacher asks her name. She begins to stammer. At last, she tells her name. The teacher encourages her. The teacher gives her a picture book. Bholi becomes happy to see all these things.

4. Does she find her teacher different from the people at home?

Answer: Yes, Bholi finds her teacher different from the people at home. At her home nobody cares for Bholi. But at school the teacher calls her name in soft and soothing voice. When she tries to tell her name, the teacher encourages her. She pats her affectionately and asks her to put the fear out of heart. This type of behaviour cannot be expected at her home.

5. Why do Bholi's parents accept Bishamber's marriage proposal?

Answer: Bholi's parents accept Bishamber's marriage proposal because they think if they don't accept it nobody will marry her in future. Though he is of forty or forty five but he is not asking for any dowry. It is a good proposal for Ramlal and his wife.

6. Why does the marriage not take place?

Answer: The marriage did not take place, because Bholi refused to marry Bishamber. When the groom saw that her face was covered with pock marks, he demanded a dowry of five thousand rupees. Bholi's father requested to accept rupees two thousand. But Bishamber was adamant. To see all these, Bholi decided not to marry such a greedy man.

6. Bholi was a neglected child. Explain in 30-40 words?

Answer: Bholi was a neglected child. She was neither beautiful nor intelligent. She had fallen off from her cot and damaged her brain in her childhood. She stammered when she talked. Everybody in her family thought that she was good for nothing.

Passage writing

Important points to remember :

1. Firstly, read the questions carefully and then try to find the answers.
2. Read the passage thoroughly keeping in mind the questions to be answered. The reading should be quick.
3. Whenever a relevant answer is found, underline them.
4. Normally the answers in the passage are found in a logical sequence.
5. Answers should be written in simple English using own words. Using of too long and complex sentences should be avoided.
6. In order to find out the correct option in Multiple Choice Questions, we must read all the options carefully. We should find out the most logical one.

Factual passage writing

In this part of question paper, twelve multiple Choice Questions based on a Case-based factual passage (with visual input- statistical data, chart etc.) of 300-350 words will be given. This is to test analysis and interpretation capabilities of the students. Students may be asked to answer ten out of these twelve questions.

1. Read the passage given below and answer the questions/complete the sentences that follow: 8 Marks

A chimpanzee is one of the great apes and the nearest in intelligence to man. Scientists have examined its mental capacities and sent it into space in anticipation of man. Chimpanzees need little description. Being apes and not monkeys, they have no tails. Their arms are longer than their legs and they normally rim on all fours. They can also walk upright with toes turned outwards. When erect they stand 3-5 ft high. The hair is long and coarse, black except for a white patch near the rump. The face, ears, hands and feet are bare and except for the black face, the flesh is coloured.

Chimpanzees exhibit great concern for each other. When chimpanzees meet after having been apart they greet each other in a very human way by touching each other or even clasping hands. Chimpanzees have amazing social discipline. When a dominant male arrives, the rest of the chimpanzees hurry to pay respect to it. The dominant male is not allowed to wrest food from his inferiors. The members of a party also spend considerable amount of time grooming each other and themselves. Mothers go through the fur of their babies for any foreign particles, dirt, and ticks and they aid each other when they are injured.

Chimpanzees are the best tools users apart from man. Sticks 2-3 ft long are picked off the ground or broken from branches and pushed into nests, then withdrawn and the honey or insects licked off. Stones are used to crack nuts or as missiles to drive humans and baboons away from its food. Chimpanzees are not only tool users but also toolmakers. They make their own rods by stripping the leaves off a twig or tear shreds off a grass stem. Baby chimpanzees learn all this by observing the older chimpanzees making and using them. So man is not the easily toolmaker, merely better at it than his relatives.

(a) Chimpanzees are as_______ as men.
(b) Chimpanzees greet each other by_______ each other.
(c) Like man, chimpanzees are_______.
(d) Chimpanzees_______ tails.
(e) Baby chimpanzees learn, all by _______.
(f) Chimpanzees have amazing _______.
(g) The dominant male chimpanzees is not allowed _______.
(h) The word 'wrest' means_______.

Answer: (a) intelligent.
(b) touching.
(c) both tool users and toolmakers.
(d) have no.
(e) observing the older chimpanzees.
(f) social discipline.
(g) to take food from inferiors.
(h) to take away violently.

2. Read the passage given below and answer the questions/complete the sentences that follow: 8 Marks

A sparrow is a small bird which is found throughout the world. There are many different species of sparrows. Sparrows are only about four to six inches in length. Many people appreciate their beautiful song. Sparrows prefer to build their nests in low places-usually on the ground, clumps of grass, low trees and low bushes. In cities they build their nests in building nooks or holes. They rarely build their nests in high places. They build their nests out of twigs, grasses and plant fibers. Their nests are usually small and well-built structures.

Female sparrows lay four to six eggs at a time. The eggs are white with reddish brown spots. They hatch between eleven to fourteen days. Both the male and female parents care for the young. Insects are fed to the young after hatching. The large feet of the sparrows are used for scratching seeds. Adult sparrows mainly eat seeds. Sparrows can be found almost everywhere, where there are humans. Many people throughout the world enjoy these delightful birds.

The sparrows are some of the few birds that engage in dust bathing. Sparrows first scratch a hole in the ground with their feet, then lie in it and fling dirt or sand over their bodies with flicks of their winds. They also bathe in water, or in dry or melting snow. Water bathing is similar to dust bathing, with the sparrow standing in shallow water and flicking water over its back with its wings, also ducking its head under the water. Both activities are social, with up to a hundred birds participating at once, and is followed by preening and sometimes group singing.

(a) The chief food for the adult sparrow is _________.
(b) Sparrows live wherever _________
(c) The word, 'species' means_________
(d) Sparrows _________ in high places.
(e) _________ take care of the young sparrows.
(f) Sparrows take bathe in _________
(g) Bathing for the sparrows is a _________
(h) Bathing is followed by_________ and_________

Answer:

(a) seeds.
(b) there are humans.
(c) kinds.
(d) rarely build their nests.
(e) Both parents.
(f) dust, water Or snow.
(g) social activity.
(h) preening and group singing.

Discursive passage writing

In this part twelve multiple Choice Questions based on a discursive passage of 400-450 words will be there to test inference, evaluation and vocabulary. Ten out of these twelve questions are to be answered.

1. Read the passage given below and answer the questions/complete the statements that follow 12 marks

Long, long ago, in a big forest, there were many trees. Among the cluster of trees, there was a very tall pine tree. He was so tall that he could talk to the stars in the sky. He could easily look over the heads of the other trees. One day late in the evening, the pine tree saw a ragged, skinny girl approaching him. He could see her only because of his height. The little girl was in tears. The pine tree bent as much as he could and asked her : "What is the matter ? Why are you crying?"

The little girl, still sobbing, replied, "I was gathering flowers for a garland for goddess Durga, who I believe, would help my parents to overcome their poverty and I have lost my way". The pine tree said to the little girl, "It is late in the evening. It will not be possible for you to return to your house, which is at the other end of the forest. Sleep for the night at this place." The pine tree pointed out to an open cave-like place under him. The little girl was frightened of wild animals. The girl quickly crept into the cave-like place. The pine tree was happy and pleased with himself. He stood like a soldier guarding the place. The little girl woke up in the morning and was amazed to see the pine tree standing guard outside the cave. Then her gaze travelled to the heap of flowers that she had gathered the previous night. The flowers lay withering on the ground. The pine tree understood what was going on in the girl's mind. He wrapped his branches around the nearby flower trees and shook them gently. The little girl's eyes brightened. But a great surprise awaited her. The pine tree brought out a bag full of gold coins which had been lying for years in the hole in its trunk and gave it to the girl. With teary eyes she thanked her benefactor and went away.

(A) Answer the following questions: **Marks 8 (2 x 4)**

(i) Why was the girl crying?
(ii) Where did the pine tree want the little girl to sleep for the night?
(iii) Why was the little girl disappointed when she looked at the flowers and what did the tree do to make her happy?
(iv) What lesson does this short story teach us?

(B) Do as directed: **Marks 4**

(i) What is meant by the word 'cluster' ? (Para 1)
(a) group (b) team (c) class (d) party
(ii) What is meant by the word 'approaching' ? (Para 1)
(a) calling (b) touching (c) coming close (d) running towards
(iii) What is meant by the word 'wild' ? (Para 2)
(a) cunning (b) dirty (c) unpolished (d) dangerous
(iv) What is meant by the word ' withering ' ? (Para 2)
(a) dead (b) shrunk (c) colourless (d) unhappy

Answer:

(A) (i) The little girl was gathering flowers for a garland to offer goddess Durga but she lost her way to home and she was crying out of fear.

(ii) The pine tree wanted the little girl to sleep in an open cave-like place under the tree.

(iii) When the little girl saw that the flowers that she had gathered the previous night laid withered on the ground, she got disappointed. The tree wrapped his branches around the nearby flower trees and shook them gently so that the little girl can collect enough flower and she can become happy.

(iv) The short story teaches us that those who have faith in god can overcome any trouble.

(B) (i) (a) group.
(ii) (c) coming close.
(iii) (c) unpolished.
(iv) (a) dead.

Grammar

Tenses

What is tense?

A tense may be defined as that form of a verb which indicates the time and the state of an action or event.Tense is firstly classified into three types- past tense, present tense, and future tense.

Present Tense

This form of tense refers to action taking place in the present time.

Types of Present Tense:

1. Present Indefinite Tense
2. Present Continuous Tense
3. Present Perfect Tense
4. Present Perfect Continuous Tense

Present Indefinite Tense

This tense is generally used to denote habit, custom, practice, repeated action, permanent activity, general truth etc. Also, it is used to make a statement in the present showing permanent nature and activity of the subject.

Example- a) The earth moves round the sun.

b) Nilesh always gets up early in the morning.

RULES:

AFFIRMATIVE – Subject + Main Verb + s/es + Object.

NEGATIVE – Subject + do/does + not + Main Verb + Object.

INTERROGATIVE – Do/does + Subject + Main Verb + object + ?

Present Continuous Tense

This tense is generally used for an action in progress that is temporary in nature in the present at the time of speaking.

Example- The teacher is teaching them English.

It also expresses future action or a definite arrangement in the near future.

Example- I am going to visit the doctor tomorrow.

RULES:

AFFIRMATIVE – Subject + is/am/are + Main Verb + ing + Object.

NEGATIVE – Subject + is/am/are + not + Main Verb + ing + Object.

INTERROGATIVE – Is/am/are + Subject + Main Verb + ing + Object + ?

Present Perfect Tense

This tense generally indicates an action that has been completed sometime before the present moment, with a result that affects the present situation.

Example-
The students have left the hostel.

RULES:

AFFIRMATIVE – Subject +has/have + IIIrd form of Verb + Object.

NEGATIVE – Subject + has/have + not + IIIrd form of Verb + Object.

INTERROGATIVE – Has/Have + Subject + IIIrd form of Verb + object + ?

Present Perfect Continuous Tense

This tense generally indicates an action that started in the past and is still continuing at the present time.
Example- It has been raining since morning.

RULES:

AFFIRMATIVE – Subject +has/have + been + Main Verb + ing + Object + for/since + period/time.

NEGATIVE – Subject +has/have + not been + Main Verb + ing + Object + for/since + period/time.

INTERROGATIVE –Has/have + subject + been + Main Verb + ing + Object + for/since + period/time + ?

Past Tense

This form of tense indicates the happening or non-happening of an action or event in the past time.

Types of Past Tense:

1. Past Indefinite Tense
2. Past Continuous Tense
3. Past Perfect Tense
4. Past Perfect Continuous Tense

Past Indefinite Tense

This tense is generally used as a part of a habit. Also, it is used for a single act completed in past.

Example- a) Riju started a new business last year.

b) Aijul did not like coffee.

RULES:

AFFIRMATIVE

Subject + IInd form of Verb + Object.

Or

Subject + IInd form of Helping Verb + Main Verb+ Object.

NEGATIVE – Subject + did + not + Main Verb + Object.

INTERROGATIVE – Did + Subject + Main Verb + object + ?

Past Continuous Tense

This tense is generally used for past action in progress that is temporary in nature in the present at the time of speaking.

Example- He was reading a novel when I reached his home.

It also expresses a definite arrangement for the future in the past.

Example- Arup was going to meet his younger brother.

RULES:

AFFIRMATIVE – Subject + was/were + Main Verb + ing + Object.

NEGATIVE – Subject + was/were + not + Main Verb + ing + Object.

INTERROGATIVE – was/were + Subject + Main Verb + ing + Object + ?

Past Perfect Tense

This tense generally indicates an action in the past that had been completed before another time or event in the past.

Example-

The train had left before we reached the station.

RULES:

AFFIRMATIVE – Subject +had + IIIrd form of Verb + Object.

NEGATIVE – Subject + had + not + IIIrd form of Verb + Object.

INTERROGATIVE – Had + Subject + IIIrd form of Verb + object + ?

Past Perfect Continuous Tense

This tense generally indicates an action in the past that took place before another time or event in the past and continued during the second event/time point in the past.

Example-
It had been raining for three days when we reached Manali.

RULES:

AFFIRMATIVE – Subject +had + been + Main Verb + ing + Object + for/since + period/time.

NEGATIVE – Subject +had + not been + Main Verb + ing + Object + for/since + period/time.

INTERROGATIVE –Had + subject + been + Main Verb + ing + Object + for/since + period/time + ?

Future Tense

This form of tense indicates the happening or non-happening of an action or event in the future time.

Types of Future Tense:

1. Future Indefinite Tense
2. Future Continuous Tense
3. Future Perfect Tense
4. Future Perfect Continuous Tense

Future Indefinite Tense

This tense is generally used to indicate an action that will take place after the present time and that has no real connection with the present time.

Example-
They will come tomorrow.

RULES:

AFFIRMATIVE – Subject +will/shall + I^{st} form of Verb + s/es + Object.

NEGATIVE – Subject + will/shall + not + Main Verb + Object.

INTERROGATIVE – Will/Shall + Subject + Main Verb + object + ?

Future Continuous Tense

This tense is generally used for an action that will be in progress with a point of time in future.

Example- Sarat will be playing by this time tomorrow.

It also expresses definite future arrangement.

Example- You will be sitting in the examination hall tomorrow.

RULES:

AFFIRMATIVE – Subject + will/shall + be + Main Verb + ing + Object.

NEGATIVE – Subject + will/shall + not be + Main Verb + ing + Object.

INTERROGATIVE – Will/Shall + Subject + Main Verb + ing + Object + ?

Future Perfect Tense

This tense generally indicates an action in the future that will have been completed before another time or event in the future.

Example-
I will have searched him out before sunset.

RULES:

AFFIRMATIVE – Subject +will/shall + have + IIIrd form of Verb + Object.

NEGATIVE – Subject + will/shall +not + have + IIIrd form of Verb + Object.

INTERROGATIVE – Will/Shall+ Subject + have been + IIIrd form of Verb + object +?

Future Perfect Continuous Tense

This tense generally indicates an action in the future that will have been continuing until another time or event in the future.

Example-

Harish will have been cleaning the lawn when you will meet him.

RULES:

AFFIRMATIVE – Subject +will/shall + have been + Main Verb + ing + Object + for/since + period/time.

NEGATIVE – Subject +will/shall + not + have been + Main Verb + ing + Object + for/since + period/time.

INTERROGATIVE – Will/Shall + subject + have been + Main Verb + ing + Object + for/since + period/time + ?

Use the correct tense form of the verbs given in brackets

(1) Father is not at home; he ____ out (go)
(2) He ____ the station before the train departed. (reach)
(3) It's time we ____ home. (return)
(4) The new teacher ____ us now for six months. (teacher)
(5) Mohan ____ home before it started raining. (reach)
(6) He told us that he never ____ a lie (tell)
(7) Our teacher ____ to London last year. (go)
(8) John ____ a number of short stories.(write)
(9) We should never ____ a lie. (tell)
(10) The lady slipped while she (climb) the steps.
(11) We shall wait here until he (come) back.
(12) He talks as if he (know) everything.
(13) He jumped off the bus while it ____. (move)
(14) He said that he ____ the letter. (post)
(15) He ____ a teacher since 1994. (be)
(16) We (know) each other for five years.
(17) The other day I (meet) a magician in the market.
(18) She said that she (will) help her friend.
(19) The boys (play) in the garden when the tree fell down.
(20) I wish I (be) a king.
(21) The boy (sleep), don't disturb him.
(22) She ____ a book when I saw her. (read)

(23) She ____ a teacher since 2002. (be)
(24) The bell rang after we (finish) our work.
(25) Please ring me up as soon as he (come).
(26) It is time we (go) to bed.
(27) She behaves as if she (know) everything.
(28) If it (rain) we shall not go out.
(29) We (know) each other for the last ten years.
(30) If I (be) you, I would not have called him again.
(31) The Principal is not in his room. He (go) out.
(32) Elephants (be verb) the largest land mammals.
(33) Three species of elephants (live) living today.

Answer:

(1) Father is not at home; he has gone out.
(2) He had reached the station before the train departed.
(3) It's time we returned home.
(4) The new teacher has been teaching us now for six months.
(5) Mohan had reached home before it started raining.
(6) He told us that he never tells a lie.
(7) Our teacher went to London last year.
(8) John has written a number of short stories.
(9) We should never tell a lie.
(10)The lady slipped while she climbed the steps.
(11)We shall wait here until he comes back.
(12)He talks as if he knew everything.
(13)He jumped off the bus while it moved.
(14)He said that he had posted the letter.
(15) He has been a teacher since 1994.
(16)We have known each other for five years.
(17)The other day I met a magician in the market.
(18)She said that she would help her friend.
(19)The boys were playing in the garden when the tree fell down.
(20)I wish I were a king.
(21)The boy is sleeping, don't disturb him.
(22)She was reading a book when I saw her.
(23)She has been a teacher since 2002.
(24)The bell rang after we had finished our work.
(25)Please ring me up as soon as he comes.
(26)It is time we went to bed.
(27)She behaves as if she knew everything.
(28)If it rains, we shall not go out.
(29) We have known each other for the last ten years.
(30) If I were you, I would not have called him again.
(31)The Principal is not in his room. He has gone out.
(32)Elephants are the largest land mammals.
(33)Three species of elephants are living living today.

Modals

A modal verb is a type of verb that is used to indicate modality, that is, ability, capacity, permission, request, order, suggestion etc. The commonly used modal verbs are- can, could, may, might, must, will, shall, should, ought to, need etc.

Important points to be noted

1. Modal verbs are generally used in the present tense. In the third person singular number, 's' or 'es' is not used.

   Example:
   Sheema must go to your home. (Here we cannot use musts)

2. In negative sentences, no helping verb is required.

   Example:
   Ashok should not do that.

   Niran need not go to his office every day.

3. Modal verbs are always used along with a main verb. This not applicable in case of Tag questions and very short reply.

   Example:

   You may come anytime at noon.

   I can go home alone.

Here, 'come' and 'go' are main verbs.

Common Modal Verbs

Can, Could, May, Might, Must/ Ought to, Shall, Should, Will, Would.

Subject – Verb Concord

Before understanding the topic Subject-Verb concord we must understand the terms 'Subject' and 'Verb'. 'Subject' in a sentence is the noun or pronoun about which the sentence tells us. On the other hand, 'Verb' is the action in the sentence. Now, we come to the topic Subject-Verb concord. 'Concord' means agreement. When the subject and verb in a sentence do not match or agree, the sentence cannot be proper. Even the sentence cannot carry the meaning it was meant for.

Rule 1.

The verb and subject must agree in number (singular or plural). If the subject is singular, the verb should be singular in number. Again, if the subject is in plural, the verb should also be in plural.

Example-

1. She lives in Chennai.

Since, the subject 'she' is in singular form, singular form of the verb 'live', i.e., 'lives' has been used.

2. They live in a small hut.

Since, the subject 'they' is in plural form, plural form of the verb 'live' has been used.

Rule 2.

The number of the subject will not change due to words/phrases in between the subject and the verb.

Example-

Each of the boys was intelligent.

In this sentence, the subject is 'each', not 'the boys'. So, the verb 'was' is in singular form.

Rule 3.

If the subjects are joined by ‘and’ in a sentence, a plural verb will be used. But, if subjects are joined by ‘either/or’, ‘neither/nor’, a singular verb will be used.

Examples:

1. Nitu and Rana are playing in the field.

2. Either Ritesh or Bhabesh is coming today.

Rule 4.

The verb in a sentence containing ‘or’, ‘either/or’, ‘neither/nor’ agrees with the noun or pronoun closest to it.

Example:

Neither he nor his parents are coming to the meeting.

In this sentence, two subjects are there, but the verb ‘are’ agrees with the closest subject, ‘his parents’.

Rule 5.

When the subject is followed by words such as ‘as well as’, ‘along with’, ‘besides’, etc. ignore them and use a singular verb if the subject is singular.

Example:

Jon, as well as his brother, is coming to our home.

Rule 6.

In sentences that begin with ‘here’, ‘there’, the true subject usually follows the verb.

Examples:

2. There is a tall building near the police station.
3. There are several water falls in Meghalaya.

Rule 7.

In sentences that include sums of money, periods of time or distances etc. (as a unit), use singular verbs.

Example:

92 rupees is a good price for your book.

Rule 8.

In the case of words such as 'a lot of', 'all', 'some' etc. in a sentence, pay attention to the noun after 'of'. If the noun after 'of' is singular then use a singular verb, if plural use a plural verb.

Examples:

1. All of the buffaloes were driven off.

2. All of the pizza is eaten by them.

Rule 9.

In sentences where collective nouns such as group, population etc. are there, the verb will be either singular or plural depending upon their uses.

Examples:

1. Most of the population is not supporting the Act.

2. Most of the population are not supporting the Act.

It is interesting to see that both the above sentences are correct.

Rule 10.

Some words like mathematics, news etc are plural in form but these are singular in meaning. So, singular verbs will be used.

Examples:

1. Mathematics is an important subject.

2. The news is spread very fast.

1. Fill in the blank with the most suitable auxiliary verb.

a. Each of the boys ________________given a prize by the chief guest. (did/is/does/was)

b. Ninety rupees ________________too much for this bag. (have/were/is/are)

c. Somebody in the library group always ____________________ to bring the book. (have/has/forgets/forget)

Answer:

a. was
b. is
c. forgets

Direct and Indirect Speech

The way of reporting the words of a speaker is called Narration. There are two main ways of reporting the words of a speaker-

1. Direct Speech
2. Indirect Speech

Direct Speech

In this form, the actual words of the speaker are put within quotation mark.
For example- Arun said, "She is not coming today."

In this sentence, 'Arun' is the **Reporter**, 'said' is the **Reporting Verb** and "She is not coming today" is the **Reported speech**.

Indirect Speech

To report speaker's Speech to another person in our own words without changing the meaning of the Speech is known as Indirect Speech or Indirect Narration.

For example- Milon told me that he was seriously ill that day.

Basic rules to convert a Direct Speech to Indirect Speech.

The following are the basic rules to convert a Direct speech to an Indirect speech.

1. To change the reporting verb according to the reported speech.
2. To remove the inverted comma's from the direct speech and replace them with an appropriate conjunction.
3. To change the pronoun of reported speech accordingly.
4. Change the adverbs of the Direct Speech.

Direct - Nitin said to me, "I have nothing to say"
Indirect - Nitin told me that he had nothing to say.

Here in this example,

Reporting verb 'said to' is changed into 'told'.
Inverted Commas are replaced by the conjunction that
Reported speech's pronoun I is changed into 'he'.
Reported speech's verb 'have' is changed into 'had'.

Rules to change Reported Speech

Rule No 1.

1st Person pronoun of Reported speech is changed according to the Subject of Reporting verb.

Direct Speech: Binita says, "I am older than Nitu."
Indirect Speech: Binita says that she is older than Nitu.

Direct Speech: Gautam says, "I am reading a novel"
Indirect Speech: Gautam says that he is reading a novel.

Rule No 2.

2nd Person pronoun of Reported speech is changed according to Object of Reporting verb.

Direct Speech: Karan says to me, "You should come early"
Indirect Speech: Karan tells me that I should go early.

Direct Speech: Neelav says to her, "You are successful"
Indirect Speech: Neelav tells her that she is successful.

Direct Speech: I say to them, "You should remain silent."
Indirect Speech: I tell them that they should remain silent.

Rule No 3.

3rd Person Pronoun of Reported speech is not changed.

Direct Speech: Anupam says, "She does not do her work sincerely"
Indirect Speech: Anupam says that she does not do her work sincerely.

Direct Speech: He says, "They have completed their assignments"
Indirect Speech: He says that they have completed their assignments.

Rules of change of verb or Tense

Rule No.1

If reporting verb is given in Present or Future tense then there will be no change in the verb or tense of Reported speech

Direct Speech: My father says, "She makes the ceremony a grand success".
Indirect Speech: My father says that she makes the ceremony a grand success.

Direct Speech: Anil is saying, "Everybody in the house is safe".
Indirect Speech: Anil is saying that everybody in the house is safe.

Direct Speech: Max will say, "Luciana is doing well".
Indirect Speech: Max will say that Luciana is doing well.

Rule No.2

If reporting verb is given in Past tense then the tense of the verb of Reported Speech will change into corresponding Past tense.

Direct Speech: The old man said, "I am collecting some old photos."
Indirect Speech: The old man said that he was collecting some old photos.

Direct Speech: Ruchika said to me, "He has already left".
Indirect Speech: Ruchika told me that he had already left.

Corresponding Changes to past form in an indirect speech from the verb in Reported speech.

1. **Simple present** changes to **Simple Past**
2. **Present Continuous** changes to **Past Continuous**
3. **Present Perfect** changes to **Past Perfect**
4. **Present Perfect Continuous** changes to **Past Perfect Continuous**
5. **Simple Past** changes to **Past Perfect**
6. **Past Continuous** changes to **Past Perfect Continuous**
7. **In Future Tense will/Shall** changes to **would**
8. **Can** changes to **Could**

9. **May** changes to **Might**

Exceptions of this rule-

Exception case I.

If the direct speech indicates a 'Universal Truth' or 'Habitual action' then there will be no change in the Tense form.

Direct Speech: My father said, "The earth moves round the sun."
Indirect Speech: My father said that the earth moves round the sun. (Universal Truth)

Direct Speech: Mayank said to me, "I do my homework myself."
Indirect Speech: Mayank told me that he does his homework himself. (Habitual fact)

Exception case II.
If the direct speech indicates any Past Historical Fact then there will be no change in the Tense form.

Direct Speech: Sanjay said, "Akbar died in 1605 AD."
Indirect Speech: Sanjay said that Akbar died in 1605 AD.

Exception case III.
If the direct speech has two actions happening at a time, then there will be no change in the Tense form.

Direct Speech: Richa said "I was doing my homework when my brother was having lunch"
Indirect Speech: Richa said that she was doing her homework when her brother was having lunch.

Exception case IV.

If the direct speech has some Imagined Condition then there will be no change in the Tense form.

Direct Speech: Ritesh said, "If I were rich, I would help her."
Indirect Speech: Ritesh said that if he were rich he would help her.

Exception case V.

If the direct speech contains had 3rd form, to-infinitive and would, could, should, must, might, ought to etc. then there will be no change in the Tense form.

Direct Speech: Nilakshi said to me, "Nobody should harm the others."
Indirect Speech: Nilakshi told me that nobody should harm the others.

The following words are changed as given while changing Direct Speech to Indirect Speech.

DIRECT	INDIRECT
Here	There
Now	Then
This	That
These	Those
Today	That day
To-night	That night
Yesterday	The previous day
Last night	The previous night
Last week	The previous week
Tomorrow	The next day
Next Week	The following week
Ago	Before
Thus	So
Hence	Thence
Hither	Thither
Come	Go

Interrogative sentences

Rules to change Direct speech to Indirect Speech

Rule 1.

In case of an interrogative sentences of Yes/No type, if/whether is used instead of that.

Example: Direct Speech: Robin said to Nilotpal, "Are you appearing in the exams?"
Indirect Speech: Robin asked Nilotpal if he was appearing in the exams.

Rule 2.

In case of a 'Wh' type question, the connector 'that' is not used.

Example: Direct Speech: He said to Anil, "When are you coming to my place?"
Indirect Speech: He asked when he was going to his place.

Rule 3.

It is very important to note that the structure of the indirect speech is always an Assertive sentence and it is as given below-
Subject + Helping Verb + Verb + Object

Imperative Sentences

Imperative sentences are those sentences which indicate advice, order, request or suggestion etc.

Rules to change Direct speech to Indirect Speech

Rule 1.

When the reported speech of direct narration is with imperative sentence, the reporting verb 'say' is changed to 'order', 'beg', 'advise', 'demand' etc. depending on the meaning of the imperative sentence.

Example: Direct Speech: The teacher said to Riwaj, "Come to the library".
Indirect Speech: The teacher ordered Riwaj to go to the library.
Direct Speech: The old lady said to Nita, "Please help me to cross the road".
Indirect Speech: The old lady requested Nita to help her to cross the road.

Rule 2.

In order to change the reported speech with such imperative sentence, 'to' is used as connector in place of 'that'.

Example: Direct Speech: The teacher said to Anil, "Do your homework neatly"
Indirect Speech: The teacher advised Anil to do his homework neatly.

Determiners

Determiners are the words which are used before nouns to determine or fix their meaning.

Types of Determiners

2. Articles: a/an, the.
3. Demonstrative adjectives: this, that, these, those.
4. Possessives: my, our, your, his, her, its, their.
5. Adjectives (Quantity & Number) : some, any, much, many, all, both, little, few, several, less, one, two, etc.
6. Others: each, every, next, another, either, either, first, second etc.

Definite article–

The- This is used before both countable and uncountable nouns.

Where to use:

1. When we talk about something for the second time in the same context or anything qualified by a phrase.

Example:

There was **a** little plump boy standing at my gate, **the** boy was smiling.

At the first reference 'a' is used, but at the second reference definite article 'the' is used.

2. In the Superlative Degree sentences 'the' is used before the adjectives.

Example:

She is the most beautiful girl in the class.

3. It is used before the names of water bodies. But not used before the names of lakes.

Examples:

The Ganges, The Atlantic ocean, The Red sea

4. It is used before the names of Mountain ranges. But, not used before the names of peaks.

Examples:

The Himalayas

5. 'The' is used before the names of satellites, stars, planets etc

Examples:

The moon, The earth, The sun etc.

6. 'The' is used before the names of monuments and memorials.

Examples:

The Victoria Palace, The Qutub Minar, The Taj Mahal

7. 'The' is used before the names of Scriptures or holy book.

Examples:

The Ramayana, The Mahabharata, The Bible, The Quran.

8. 'The' is used before the names of Newspapers and Magazines.

Examples:

The Times of India, The Hindu, The Guardian etc.

The man who has long hair is a carpenter.

Indefinite article–

A- It is used before singular countable nouns beginning with consonant sound.

Example-

a one-eyed man, a unique place, a European, a University, a Mango etc.

An– It is used before singular countable nouns beginning with vowel sound.

Example-

an Indian, an hour, an umbrella, an honest boy.

Demonstrative adjectives:

This- To demonstrate nearby things

That- To demonstrate far off things

These- Plural form of ‘this’

Those- Plural form of ‘that’

Possessives Determiners:

These are used to denote ownership and belongingness.

Examples:

My, our, your, his, her, its, their.

Adjectives (Quantity & Number) :

Some of the adjectives used as determiners are used only before countable nouns. For example- many, all, both, several, each, every, next another etc.

Some of the adjectives used as determiners are used only before uncountable nouns. For example- much, less etc.

Some of such determiners are used both with countable nouns and uncountable nouns. For example- Some, any, little, few, several, either, neither etc.

Complete the sentences given below by filling in the blanks choosing the correct option from those that follow-

1. **The elephant’s gestation period is 22 months, ___________ longest for any land animal. (a/ an/ which/ the)**
2. **Many guests were invited but only -----------turned up. (few/ a few/the few)**
3. **This is ---------------European lady I was talking about. (a/an/the)**
4. **I cannot give you -----------------money. (any/ few/a little)**
5. **We found the house without ____________difficulty. (many/more/much)**
6. **Sri Lanka is _____________ island. (a/an/the)**
7. **_______________of the boys was rewarded. (each/every/few)**
8. **He gave away ________________money he had to the beggar. (little/a little/the little)**
9. **Reading is ______useful hobby. (a/an/the)**
10. **Only ______________of the candidates were suitable. (few/ a few/the few)**

11. They won the game without ________________difficulty. (many/more/much)
12. ________________of the competitors will get a certificate. (each/every/few)
13. My brother is ___________N.C.C. cadet. (a/an/the)
14. First, read ______________books you have. (few/ a few/the few)
15. _____________of the oranges were rotten. (many/more/much)
16. Socrates gave ____________useful advice to his pupils. (many/more/much)
17. Hurry up! We have only ______________time left. (little/a little/the little)
18. The workers decided to form __________union. (a/an/the)
19. The painter is a man of ___________words. (few/ a few/the few)
20. _______________honorary secretary gets no salary for holding a post. (a/an/the)
21. ___________of the candidates must produce her/his identity. (each/every/few)
22. India won the match with ____________bit of luck. (little/a little/the little)
23. ______________men are free from faults. (few/ a few/the few)
24. _______________hour has passed since he left us. (a/an/the)
25. ____________of the students will be given a copy of the magazine. (each/every/few)
26. Please give me ____________money you have. (little/a little/the little)
27. He will come back within _________hour. (a/an/the)
28. ______men are free from faults. (few/ a few/the few)
29. Leap year falls in _________ fourth year. (each/every/few)
30. _________________learning is a dangerous. (little/a little/the little)
31. I gave _______one rupee note to the beggar. (a/an/the)
32. My father is ____________older than my mother. (many/more/much)
33. I buy ___________books every month. (each/every/few)
34. I need __________________money I have. (little/a little/the little)

Answer:

1. The
2. a few
3. the
4. any
5. much
6. an
7. Each
8. the little
9. a
10. a few
11. much
12. Each
13. An
14. the few
15. Many
16. Much

17. a little
18. a
19. few
20. An
21. Each
22. a little
23. Few
24. An
25. Each
26. the little
27. an
28. Few
29. Every
30. A little
31. A
32. Much
33. a few
34. the little

Letter Writing

Letter writing is an art. There are two types of letters- formal and informal letters. Different types of letters may be asked to write in the exam. Students may practice the following types of letters-

1. Letter to the editor of a news paper
2. Complaint letter
3. Order placing letter
4. Enquiry letter

Format of a Formal Letter:

The format of a formal letter should be as given below-

i. Sender's Address- The sender should write his address in the beginning of the letter on the left hand upper corner.
ii. Date- The date of writing the letter should be written below the Sender's address
iii. Receiver's Address- The address of the recipient should be written here.
iv. Subject to the letter- The purpose of the letter should be written in 5-6 words.
v. Salutation- Respected sir/madam, Dear sir/Madam etc.
vi. Body- In this part of the letter the matter of the letter is explained. In the beginning, we should introduce ourselves and the write the purpose of the letter in brief. In the next paragraph the matter should be explained in detail. In the last paragraph of the body of the letter, we should conclude the letter by giving some conclusion.
vii. Complimentary closing- In this part, the sender should include some complementary closing like- Thanking you etc., then the phrases like With regards, yours faithfully, yours sincerely etc. should be added.
viii. Sender's name and designation

1. **You are Kamal/John of 201, Block-C, Anand Vihar Coloney, New Delhi. You need an accommodation at a hotel in Manali. Write a letter to the Manager of a hotel enquiring about rent and booking of accommodation.**

   Answer:
   201, Block-C, Anand Vihar Coloney,

New Delhi.

Dated the 10th of August, 2020

The Manager,
Hotel Kanishka Grand
Manali, Madhya Pradesh.

Sub: Enquiry about the availability and booking of accommodation.

Dear sir,

I stayed in your hotel three years back, when I came to Manali on a vacation tour. It was a nice experience for us. We found the rooms quite comfortable and the location was also very good and convenient. The pick-ups and the food was excellent.

This time too, we have a plan to visit Manali along with two other families. We will reach Manali by 17th of August, 2020. We need three double bedrooms with attached bathroom for six days.

Would you please let me know if such an accommodation will be available during the mentioned period? You are also requested to let me know the room rent and other terms and conditions for availing room.

Immediately after getting your reply, I will book my rooms and plan my tour program accordingly. Hope for an early response from your end.

Thanking you

Yours faithfully
Kamal

Story Writing

Story writing is an art. Before writing the story the plot of the story should be decided. Story should be started with the given clue only. We may add something to make the starting more interesting but it should be logical. Again logical sequence of the events is also very important. The conclusion should be smooth. It should not be ended up with sudden conclusion.

Main points to remember-

1. **Title** : The title of the story should be interesting one. It is better to decide the title after finishing the story.
2. **Theme**: The story should be evolved round the central theme of the story.
3. **Correctness**: We should try to keep spelling mistakes and grammatical errors as minimum as possible. In order to make it error free we should avoid using complicated sentence pattern.
4. **Language**: The language used in the story should be simple enough, so that the common readers find it easy to understand.
5. **Characterisation**: There should be maturity in choosing the characters of the story. They should be logical and attractive to the readers. These should be well defined.
6. **Length**: The story should not be extra ordinarily long at some point. The whole story should be written in limited numbers of words. So, the flow of the story should be in a controlled way.

In the question paper first few lines will be given and the students are required to develop the story. As per current syllabus, words limit for story writing is 150-200 words.

Some examples of story writing are given below-

1. Complete the following story in 150-200 words.

Once there was an old man. He had four sons. They always quarreled with one another. One fine day…………………….. 10

Answer:

Unity is strength

Once there was an old man. He had four sons. They always quarreled with one another. One fine day, the old rich man called together his sons and told that his death is imminent. He asked them to bring a bundle of sticks. Then he asked them to break the bundle one by one.

The eldest one came and tried but nothing happened. Then it was the turn of the second boy. He also tried hard and could not. Then the third and fourth also came and tried, but all were in vain.

The rich man smiled at them and said, "Can you understand why you could not break the bundle?" They could not reply. The old man asked them to untie the bundle and break the sticks one by one. They did it easily. The old man said calmly, "It is very easy to break the sticks one by one, but when they are bundled together, it is not so easy. Likewise, if you four brothers remain together, nobody can harm you. But, if you are not united and quarrel with each other, the others can hurt you easily.

The End

www.ingramcontent.com/pod-product-compliance
Lightning Source LLC
LaVergne TN
LVHW082250150826
845677LV00009B/1594

* 9 7 9 8 5 7 5 8 2 9 3 3 1 *